THE LEGEND
OF
ARCANE

Essential Facts For Fans And A Guide Through The Making Of The Movie Series, Season 1 And 2

JEFF K. NAYLOR

Disclaimer

The content of this book is provided for informational and entertainment purposes only. While every effort has been made to ensure the accuracy of the information presented, the author makes no representations or warranties regarding the completeness, accuracy, reliability, or suitability of the information contained herein.

This book is an independent publication and is not authorised, endorsed, or sponsored by any studio, production company, or individuals associated with the intellectual properties discussed. All names, characters, logos, and other proprietary material related to the works mentioned in this book are the property of their respective owners. No copyright or trademark infringement is intended.

Table Of Contents

Introduction to Arcane

Riot Games' acclaimed animated series Arcane was born out of a potent fusion of creative innovation, storyline ambition, and gaming culture. The original idea for the series came from Christian Linke and Alex Yee, who wanted to expand and enhance the already rich League of Legends universe. Linke and Yee, both long standing Riot Games contributors, have long dreamed of a narrative that would transport League of Legends players from screens and controls to a visceral and affective experience that may strengthen their bond with the game's characters and mythology.

Fans who had only seen the game's backstories in fragmented glimpses were enthralled by Arcane's initial appearance at League of Legends' 10th anniversary celebration in 2019 through character descriptions, cutscenes, and lore-based events within the game itself. For Riot Games, whose only significant media ventures to date had been game animations, music videos, and cinematic trailers, it was a huge move. But Riot's goal was not simply another video game adaptation; they wanted to create a "full storytelling experience" that could be seen as an animated series on its own, appealing to both newbies and enthusiasts.

Riot took a unique approach. Riot decided to stick with its long-standing collaboration with Fortiche Productions, a French animation firm known for its ability to blend 2D and 3D animation methods, rather than contracting out the animation to a traditional TV animation studio. With previous collaborations, such as in-game music videos like Get Jinxed, where Arcane's adored character Jinx had her music video debut, the partnership with Fortiche has shown promise. Riot spent six years crafting Arcane's first season, making sure every frame, plot, and character was refined with the kind of attention often reserved for feature films, in recognition of Fortiche's grasp of the League world and its capacity to bring complex characters to life.

The show's creation also signalled a breakthrough in TV video game adaptations, aiming to appeal to adult viewers in a novel manner for gaming-inspired animation. While complex plots and character-rich worlds in video games often make adaptation difficult, Arcane's creators capitalised on this complexity to create a series that honours and expands upon League of Legends' rich lore. Arcane immediately stood out due to its commitment to storyline and Fortiche's innovative animation style. Riot Games CEO Nicolo Laurent discussed the unconventional approach they took with Arcane: creating an animated drama with an adult theme that would immerse viewers in a complex world full of betrayal, loyalty, and social conflict, reflecting the complexities of the game's lore.

The Universe of League of Legends

Despite being intricately woven into the League of Legends universe, Arcane stands off as a fascinating stand-alone setting, particularly for those who have never played the game. The 2009 launching of the very intricate online multiplayer game League of Legends led to the development of a vast backstory over time. Riot Games developed a large world with many different locations, each with its own distinct atmosphere, culture, and magical aspects. The "City of Progress," Piltover, and it's more sinister, industrial underbelly, Zaun, are the two very different cities in which Arcane is situated.

Piltover is known for its affluent society and scientific advancements, powered by "Hextech" technology—a blend of magic and science that allows users to harness the power of magical crystals to create innovative tools and weapons. Despite its shortcomings, this city embodies the positive aspects of growth. Beneath the glittering skyscrapers of Piltover sits a neighbourhood suffocated by crime and pollution: Zaun. Unlike its pristine counterpart, Zaun is plagued by poverty, inequality, and desperation, which push its residents into dangerous pursuits, including the use of Shimmer, a powerful but volatile substance created to enhance physical abilities at the cost of safety and sanity.

The show explores two cities' connection in great detail, telling a story of luxury vs hardship. Piltover's inhabitants largely ignore the plight of Zaun's residents, while the people of Zaun often resent and distrust Piltover's elite, whom they view as indifferent or oppressive. This societal dynamic serves as the ideal background for Arcane's story, as it tackles the implications of unrestrained ambition and the expenses of development at the expense of mankind. Key groups and people from both cities play a part in this continuous fight, including the military Enforcers of Piltover and the underworld elements of Zaun.

At the centre of Arcane are the stories of the sisters, Vi and Jinx (previously known as Powder), who symbolise the tension between these two realms. Vi embodies resilience and devotion, aiming to overcome the rift between Piltover and Zaun. In contrast, Jinx's spiral into disorder reflects the effects of pain and betrayal, as well as the toll of social indifference. Their friendship and different trajectories give an approachable entrance point for new viewers unfamiliar with League of Legends, while older players enjoy the complexity added to the characters they've grown to love in-game.

Creative Team and Production Studio

Arcane's animation studio, Fortiche Productions, contributed a distinct style and technological know-how that distinguished the series in the congested field of animated television. Fortiche's artistic approach gives Arcane a painterly, almost hand-drawn appearance that is both realistic and surreal. They are well-known for their hybrid animation technique, which blends 2D and 3D animation. In the past, the studio collaborated with Riot Games on a number of popular League of Legends-themed projects, such as the music videos for "Get Jinxed" and "Warriors," which demonstrated their ability to vividly and emotionally depict the game's champions.

Fortiche elevated their craft to new heights for Arcane. Each frame was painstakingly created, combining hand-drawn 2D components with intricate 3D character models to provide an immersive and unearthly visual experience. This graphic aesthetic enhances the emotional impact of the characters' adventures while also capturing the rugged spirit of Zaun and the futuristic beauty of Piltover. Fortiche's work in Arcane has received recognition for its ability to portray delicate emotions and nuanced expressions with this unique approach, giving the animated figures a realistic and human feel.

Riot Games and Fortiche Productions' collaboration went beyond a typical client-studio arrangement. Fortiche worked closely with Christian Linke and Alex Yee to make sure the animation enhanced the narrative. As the showrunners, Linke and Yee contributed their extensive knowledge of the League of Legends world to the animation process. In order to create a smooth fusion of story and art, they worked closely with Fortiche on every detail, from character design to scene lighting.

In addition to its technological accomplishments, Fortiche's animation style has raised the standard for animated narrative in the animation business, especially for video game-inspired work. In addition to demonstrating the possibilities of video game adaptations, Arcane's success has shown how fruitful partnerships can be when they are founded on mutual respect and a same goal.

Chapter 2

Setting And Worldbuilding

Despite their geographical proximity, the two cities that make up the Arcane world—Piltover and Zaun—differ greatly in terms of riches, morals, and looks. Piltover is a bright, thriving city known for its sophisticated culture and cutting-edge technology. Piltover, also referred to as the "City of Progress," is a representation of modernism, intellect, and aspiration. This is reflected in its architecture, which has elaborate steampunk detailing and a skyline of tall, immaculate skyscrapers. Scholars, scientists, and politicians occupy its well-paved streets, all enjoying the prosperity Piltover produces as a hub for trade and technical advancement.

Zaun, on the other hand, is an industrial, gritty undercity that is hidden in Piltover's shadow. The least fortunate live in Zaun, often known as the "Undercity." As a result of the manufacturers and chemical industries that provide electricity to both cities, the city is engulfed in heavy pollution. Zaun's citizens struggle to live in the face of poverty, illness, and crime, while Piltover thrives. The city is known for its harsh, sometimes uncontrolled climate, which inspires inventions and improvised technology that lack Piltover's sophistication but possess a tough inventiveness. Since its residents create their lives in an area that few would want to live in, Zaun is in many respects a symbol of tenacity and resistance.

Arcane's themes of inequality and strife are powerfully framed by the physical and social separation between Piltover and Zaun. Despite their mutual need, the two cities have a very imbalanced relationship. Zaun's work and resources are crucial to Piltover's prosperity, yet he doesn't gain anything from this arrangement. Much of the drama in the novel is fueled by this dynamic, as the people of Zaun become more and more dissatisfied with Piltover's exploitation and lack of interest. Vi and Jinx, the primary characters who are born in Zaun and are impacted by its harsh reality, are particularly shaped by the differences between these two cities. Characters like Jayce and Caitlyn, who enjoy the benefits of Piltover, stand in stark contrast to their experiences, underscoring the tensions that build throughout the narrative.

Science Fantasy and Steampunk Components

The series' distinctive visual and thematic identity is derived from Arcane's distinctive fusion of science fantasy and steampunk aesthetics. Traditionally, the steampunk genre blends antiquated features influenced by industrial equipment from the 19th century with sophisticated mechanical technology. This impact may be seen all across Arcane, but especially in Piltover, where the city's environment is dotted with elaborate gears, pipelines, and clockwork machinery. One of the main reasons Piltover is known as the "City of Progress" is its technical brilliance. Piltover was carefully created by the series' creators, Christian Linke and Alex Yee, in collaboration with the animation studio Fortiche. The city's cultural and intellectual refinement was reflected via the use of exquisite metallic decorations and a perfect balance between beauty and mechanisation.

The steampunk that Zaun offers, however, is rougher and less polished. Its technology is more shabby, having been pieced together from leftover components and leftovers from Piltover's inventions. Because of this, Zaun has a unique visual that presents an unruly, dirty, and chaotic subterranean environment. The hazardous mutagen Shimmer, which was produced in the city's depths, is a prominent illustration of Zaun's steampunk impact. Shimmer, which represents Zaun's inventiveness and desperation, improves physical talents but at a high cost to one's health and humanity.

Hextech, a potent combination of magic and technology that functions as a major narrative device, is another way that the series integrates scientific fantasy themes. Through Hextech, Piltover's scientists—especially Jayce and Viktor—are able to use magical forces—typically associated with fantasy—in technical situations. The balance of power in Arcane's world is altered by new weapons and technologies made possible by this blending of science and magic. Hextech is both a boon and a bane, giving its users immense power while raising moral questions about who should be in charge of it. The series' examination of ambition, morality, and the possible perils of technological advancement without ethical restriction is highlighted by Jayce and Viktor's work on Hextech.

Conflicts and Social Hierarchies

The connection between Zaun's underclass and Piltover's aristocracy clearly defines Arcane's social structure, resulting in a society full of animosity, friction, and class-based disputes. With a governing council that makes choices that impact both its own population and the people of Zaun, Piltover is a symbol of money, luxury, and power. This council, which is made up of powerful and affluent people, represents the highest level of society in the city. It sets policies and manages resources to keep Piltover prosperous at Zaun's cost.

On the other hand, the repressed and disenfranchised reside in Zaun. It is home to workers, misfits, and rebels who toil under arduous circumstances, often creating the same commodities and resources that Piltover relies on. Because Aunties see the Piltovans as oppressors who disregard their wants and rights while taking advantage of their work and lives, this class divide feeds a long-standing hostility. One of Zaun's most influential leaders, Silco, is especially resentful and is committed to securing his city's independence. The yearning of many Minutes to escape Piltover's shadow and take control of their own lives is reflected in Silco's fight for Zaun's sovereignty.

Individual characters traverse this divided society throughout the series in ways that highlight the toll that systematic inequality has on individuals. Both Vi and Jinx, who were born in Zaun, suffer from loss and adversity brought on by the harsh surroundings of the city. Characters like Jayce and Caitlyn, who were raised in Piltover and seek education and occupations without facing the same survival challenges, are compared to their lives. Through these individuals, the program examines the human cost of social hierarchy and raises the issue of whether real development is possible in a society where poverty and luxury so severely separate people.

Social problems are more than simply supporting characters in Arcane; they constitute the plot's engine and the driving force behind important characters, creating nuanced connections and moral decisions that make it difficult to distinguish between heroism and villainy. like Silco are shown in the program as both merciless and defenders of a community that has seen too much oppression. Characters like Jayce, on the other hand, who at first seek scientific development with admirable goals, start to doubt their morals when the results of their activities become clear. Arcane's criticism of societal injustice is emphasised by this interaction of viewpoints, which challenges spectators to think about the price of development when it abandons whole people.

Arcane explores ageless themes of inequity, resiliency, and power relations via the settings of Piltover and Zaun in addition to creating a visually stunning universe. Because of their distinct styles and cultures, these cities are just as much a part of the narrative as Vi, Jinx, or Jayce. They provide the ideal backdrop for a story about conflict, ambition, and the quest for freedom.

Chapter 3

Plot Summary

In the cities of Piltover and Zaun, Arcane presents spectators with a society split along lines of power, money, and technology. Zaun symbolises poverty, revolt, and survival, whereas Piltover stands for wealth, creativity, and order. A tumultuous struggle driven by political friction, intensely personal connections, and occult technology is set in motion by this glaring division. Two sisters, Vi and Jinx (previously Powder), are at the heart of the plot, and their nuanced relationship serves as the season's narrative fulcrum. The series' emotional centre and driving force is their love, which is shattered by a fatal mistake.

The tragedy that moulded Vi and Jinx is introduced in the first season: when they were little, they saw their parents killed in a bloody conflict between Piltover's enforcers and Zaunite rebels. Even as they make their way through the perilous underworld, the sisters discover a sense of family after being taken in by Vander, a protecting figure in Zaun. The quiet, however, is fleeting. Hextech, a potent kind of arcane energy that has the potential to either strengthen or weaken the divide between the two cities, is unintentionally discovered after a tragic theft. With disastrous results, this revelation sends Vi, Jinx, and their friends into a maze of decisions and repercussions. Piltover and Zaun are headed for a political and personal collision as the season intensifies tension over Hextech's potential and the attraction of power.

Vi and Jinx end themselves on different sides of a developing battle as the story goes on. While Jinx, who has been traumatised and coerced by criminal lord Silco, spirals into chaos, Vi tries to provide stability and protection for her loved ones. Their broken sisterhood serves as a metaphor for the struggle between Piltover and Zaun, emphasising themes of acceptance, loyalty, and treachery. With Jinx's last act of rebellion leaving their destiny uncertain and the Piltover Council's decision to give Zaun independence hanging in the balance, the season finale emphasises the sadness of lost innocence and the cost of unbridled ambition.

Act 1: Introduction and Insights

With hints of Piltover's opulent technology and Zaun's grim survivalism, Act 1 of Arcane establishes the framework for the universe and its people. Vi and Powder's tragic history and longing for family reunification influence their motives. Their guardian and former revolutionary, Vander, discourages Vi from choosing a violent course by emphasising moderation and diplomacy. However, Powder's urge to prove herself and Vi's sense of justice drive them to do acts that have permanent repercussions.

Vi, Powder, and their adopted brothers Mylo and Claggor attempt a perilous theft in Piltover at the start of the act, which ends in a catastrophic explosion. In addition to endangering the operation, Powder's accidental encounter with a stolen arcane crystal calls Piltover's attention to Zaun. In an attempt to protect his kids from consequences, Vander attempts to bargain with Grayson, the sympathetic Sheriff of Piltover's enforcers. Despite his best attempts, the act foreshadows the impending violent transition and emphasises Vander's declining dominance.

When his experimental work with Hextech is revealed, Piltover's young inventor Jayce Talis is also entangled in the mysterious enigma. Though it presents moral dilemmas, Jayce views Hextech as a ray of hope for Piltover, driven by recollections of a miraculous encounter that spared his life. Viktor, a modest assistant with a vision as radical as Jayce's, proves to be an unexpected friend when Jayce faces criticism from Piltover's council. Jayce and Viktor's collaboration highlights the city's potential and ambition while planting the seeds for Piltover's technological revolution.

The kidnapping of Vander by Silco, a former friend turned enemy who uses the drug Shimmer to try to control Zaun, is one of the key events of Act 1. A malevolent power with aspirations for Zaun's independence is introduced with Silco. Vi, Mylo, and Clangor launch a rescue attempt when Vander is kidnapped, unintentionally putting Powder on a collision course with her fears. Powder uses a Hextech crystal to generate an explosion in a last-ditch effort to assist, killing Mylo and Claggor and destroying Vi in the process. With Vi blaming Powder and abandoning her in a state of despair, this encounter becomes the terrible finale of Act 1. Silco takes advantage of the chance to console

Powder, which causes her to change into Jinx and go on a sinister journey.

Act 2: Disagreement and Repercussions

Act 2 begins with a changed Piltover after a number of years, where Jayce and Viktor's Hextech technology has brought about unheard-of levels of affluence. Hextech's success is shown by Piltover's celebration of Progress Day, but little is being done to close the widening divide between the wealthy in Piltover and the poor in Zaun. Those who want power and control are drawn to hextech jewels because they have the ability to power whole cities. The stakes increase as Viktor, motivated by a fatal disease, pushes the limits of Hextech experiments in an attempt to discover a cure, posing moral dilemmas about the price of scientific progress.

Jinx, a talented but erratic enforcer working under Silco's tutelage, has completely embraced her wild demeanour. She struggles with desertion and betrayal, which is reflected in her more destructive behaviours. Jinx meets Caitlyn Kiramman, a Piltover enforcer and Jayce's childhood friend, while on a mission to steal a Hextech gemstone. Kiramman starts looking into Zaun's criminal underworld. Eventually, the two women's paths cross with Vi, who has been detained in Stillwater. A journey for justice is started when Caitlyn decides to free Vi, and Vi and Caitlyn team together to fight Silco.

The reunion between Vi and Jinx is a very emotional exchange. Their prior pain reappears, with Vi being plagued by the recollection of Powder's metamorphosis and Jinx feeling deceived by Vi's seeming desertion. By "baptising" Jinx into the character and pushing her to break with her previous identity as Powder, Silco further exacerbates Jinx's instability. This deed represents Jinx's total submission to her destructive tendencies and her allegiance to Silco as a surrogate father.

The internal difficulties of the major protagonists are reflected in the outward tensions between Piltover and Zaun. As a councillor today, Jayce struggles with the political fallout from his innovations, which have turned Piltover into a target. His friendship with the astute and driven councillor Mel Medarda exposes the moral lapses and deceit among Piltover's governing elite. Their previously unshakable relationship starts to crack under the weight of their divergent views as Jayce and Viktor test the boundaries of Hextech. While

Jayce struggles with the unintended repercussions of their technical advancements, Viktor's desperation drives him to experiment with Shimmer in order to improve the Hex Core, a Hextech device that can change biological matter.

By the end of Act 2, tensions are at an all-time high. Anger between the two cities increases as Piltover imposes a blockade on Zaun. Ekko, a childhood buddy of Vi and Jinx who is now in charge of the Firelights, an anti-Silco group, faces Jinx in a pivotal bridge fight. Their altercation turns into a moving illustration of their common history and their different trajectories. As Jinx detonates a grenade, leaving Ekko injured and further entrenching her spiral into violence, the sequence, which is set against a melancholy background of memories, ends tragically.

The major protagonists reach a breaking point in Act 2's closing scenes. When a violent confrontation results in the death of a child worker, Jayce's partnership with Vi to demolish Silco's Shimmer factories highlights the ethically dubious nature of their acts and forces Jayce to face the human cost of his ambition. Vi is forced to confront the full scope of her sister's metamorphosis as Jinx's growing instability leads to Caitlyn's arrest. With each character having to face the repercussions of their decisions, Act 2 puts the characters—and the audience—on the verge of a devastating conclusion.

Chapter 4

Main Characters

Throughout Arcane, Vi, often known as Violet, shows herself to be a ferocious defender, exhibiting a fiery resilience that characterises her relationships and choices. Vi, who was raised in the difficult streets of Zaun, exemplifies the tenacity required for survival while tempering it with an unwavering devotion to her loved ones. Her unwavering spirit, physical strength, and deeply rooted sense of justice—which often puts her in danger to protect others—are her distinguishing characteristics. She feels a natural need to protect Powder (later known as Jinx) as the elder sister, a duty that is made more difficult by Powder's vulnerability.

Vi's relationships are complicatedly shaped by her protective tendencies. She makes it her mission to be a mentor to Powder, her younger sister, supporting her potential and providing comfort when she feels insecure. But this also creates conflict since Vi's unflinching harshness may overwhelm Powder's brittle sense of value. As Vi learns responsibility and self-control from her adoptive father, Vander, their interactions further highlight her character. Vander has had a significant impact, and his passing motivates Vi to continue his legacy in Zaun despite her own emotions of betrayal and desertion.

Vi faces several difficult and very intimate challenges to her protective nature. Vi is forced to face the boundaries of her authority when a robbery goes horribly wrong and her closest friends and family are killed. She calls her sister a "jinx" and holds her responsible for the catastrophe, shattering her relationship with Powder. Vi is horrified and plagued by guilt as a result of her outburst, particularly when Powder eventually transforms into Jinx, an unidentifiable symbol of chaos brought on by Silco. Vi's path involves between forgiveness and retribution, trying to rescue her sister, and confronting her part in Jinx's metamorphosis.

Vi is a fierce combatant because of her physical prowess and fighting abilities, but what really sets her apart is her moral fortitude. Vi's protective instincts go beyond family connections, demonstrating her ability to fight for justice on a global scale as she joins up with Caitlyn, a Piltover enforcer, to face Silco and save Jinx. Her relationship with Caitlyn, which is based on empathy and respect for one another, gives her a fresh sense of direction and serves as a reminder that life goes on after her losses. Vi's path demonstrates the strength of her character despite her difficult trials, as she manages to balance her responsibilities as a survivor, a warrior, and a sister.

The Rebel Jinx

The erratic core of Arcane, Powder (later renamed Jinx) represents tragedy, turmoil, and revolt. She undergoes a profoundly personal metamorphosis from the naive, wide-eyed Powder to the insane and destructive Jinx, driven by pain, abandonment, and a quest for identity. She is charming but frail as Powder, and others around her often ignore or undervalue her. She aspires to show herself and seeks her sister Vi's favour, making her an idol. Nevertheless, Powder's fears and shortcomings at critical junctures result in a string of terrible errors that end in the tragedy that kills her family.

Silco's influence, who takes on the role of a substitute father figure after Powder's split from Vi, marks the change into Jinx. By fostering her darker tendencies, Silco successfully breaks her bonds with her past self. With his help, Jinx develops a persona that is both frightening and unexpected by embracing her potential for violence and mayhem. By using theatrical mayhem and weaponized creativity, she adopts a perverted form of her sister's rebellious attitude. Her internalised anger and a frantic desire to be seen, even if it is via terror, are reflected in her usage of weapons, which are often makeshift and destructive.

Even in her changed condition, Jinx's bond with Vi continues to be fundamental to who she is and influences her behaviour. Her unresolved emotions for Vi haunt her and often cause her to have hallucinations of her sister and her old self. Their connection is a complicated mixture of love, jealousy, and hatred. Even though Jinx has accepted her new identity, she is haunted by Powder's memories, and her encounters with Vi reawaken old scars that Silco's manipulations were unable to heal. The conflict she faces between the affection she experienced as a kid and the rage she has as an adult is symbolised by the contrast between Powder and Jinx.

Jinx's development throughout the series is a terrible decline, with her erratic demeanour overshadowing her moments of tenderness. Because of her erratic inclinations, she alienates anybody who tries to contact her, reflecting the severe effects of abandonment. Jinx's need for approval drives her to make a painful decision in her last encounter with Vi: either she embraces the turmoil that has made her Jinx or she clings to her sister's affection. This development makes Jinx one of Arcane's most interesting characters by highlighting her complexity as a person divided between rebellion and a deep-seated longing for connection.

Important Characters in Support

Supporting characters provide complexity to Arcane by contributing distinct motives, conflicts, and emotional depths that improve the main plot and have an impact on Vi and Jinx's adventures.

Silco: The main adversary, Silco was formerly Vander's buddy and has a similar history of betrayal and ideological differences. Aspiring and brutal, Silco will stop at nothing to secure Zaun's independence, even if it means upending Piltover.

Because he takes Jinx into his family, he fosters her rage and sees her as the daughter he never had, making their connection especially complicated. As the perverted father figure who feeds Jinx's metamorphosis, Silco has a significant impact on her by both empowering and taking advantage of her rebellious tendencies. In stark contrast to Vander's more protective demeanour, his readiness to control and sacrifice people in order to realise his vision of Zaun exemplifies the darker side of leadership.

Jayce Talis: A gifted inventor from Piltover, Jayce's quest for advancement via Hextech technology is both a blessing and a hardship. He starts off as an idealistic figure who wants to utilise magic to make Piltover prosperous, but as he rises through the ranks of politics and power, he shows the difficulties of ambition and moral ambiguity. His collaboration with Viktor, which pushes the limits of technology with unexpected effects, exemplifies the conflicts between morality and innovation. Through his friendship with Mel Medarda, Jayce is exposed to the intricacies of Piltover's elite and is compelled to negotiate a society where choices are influenced by politics. As he gains authority, Jayce finds it difficult to strike a balance between the advancement of technology and how it affects the weak, and he eventually starts to wonder how much his creations cost.

A Piltover enforcer with a strong sense of justice, Caitlyn Kiramman is motivated by her desire to learn the truth about Zaun's criminal underworld. As she exposes herself to viewpoints outside of Piltover's insulated sphere, her relationship with Vi becomes a pillar of her personality. Caitlyn is one of Vi's few reliable friends because of her empathy and wisdom, which enable her to look beyond appearances. Caitlyn and Vi have a respectful and developing relationship in which she challenges Vi's beliefs while upholding her own dedication to fairness. Caitlyn's desire to walk into Zaun, which contrasts with her aristocratic heritage, represents her open-mindedness and her dedication to bridge the gap between Piltover and its undercity.

Viktor: Jayce's innovation partner, Viktor, is a multifaceted individual distinguished by his mental aspirations and physical weakness. Viktor, a native of Zaun, offers a distinct viewpoint to the Piltover universe, questioning its principles while looking for a way over his own physical constraints. Viktor's alliance with Jayce symbolises the possibility of Piltover and Zaun coming together, but his desperate attempts to recover from his sickness push him to try out dangerous Shimmer and Hexcore technological experiments. His slow metamorphosis highlights the sad nature of ambition as his desire to have a positive impact on society clashes with his previous ethical convictions. Viktor's path illustrates the fine line between brilliance and arrogance and the moral cost of advancement.

Vander: As the surrogate father of Vi and Powder, Vander is a pillar of support who personifies kindness and defence. In contrast to Silco's hardline approach, Vander, the leader of Zaun, chooses diplomacy over violence, serving as a balancing factor. He plays a crucial part in Vi and Powder's early growth as a father figure, teaching them self-control and devotion. The death of Vander is a turning point in Zaun's life since it leaves a hole in him and compels Vi to take on a protective role that eventually alters her course. He leaves a lasting impression on the folks that follow him because of Vi's tenacity and the morals he taught.

Since their decisions and relationships have a direct influence on Vi and Jinx's life, defining their identities and paths, these ancillary characters give Arcane's story more depth. The universe of opposing principles and personal conflicts created by Silco's vicious ambition, Jayce's internal turmoil, Caitlyn's commitment to justice, and Viktor's moral dilemmas reflects the larger themes of identity, allegiance, and power. Arcane is a complicated and emotionally stirring tale because of the alliances and animosities that they weave together to show the stakes in Piltover and Zaun.

Chapter 5

Character Arcs and Development

The complicated and broken connection between sisters Vi and Jinx, who were both born Powder, is at the centre of Arcane. Their closeness is put to the test by trauma, grief, and conflicting beliefs. Their transformation from loving siblings to enmity is a powerful statement on trust, loyalty, and the high cost of violence. When Vi, Powder, and their adopted siblings Mylo and Claggor are placed in the custody of Vander, a fatherly figure in Zaun, early in the book, this relationship is formed. As Powder's elder sister, Vi is very protective of her and is often comforting her when their friends make fun of her. Though she suffers with self-doubt, sometimes doubting her talents and feeling like a burden to her elder sister, Powder idolises Vi and aspires to her praise.

The catastrophe that defines their life and the pivotal moment in their relationship occurs after a failed mission in Piltover. Powder uses a stolen magical stone to try to assist Vi and their friends get out of a dangerous position, but the scheme fails. Mylo and Claggor are killed in the ensuing explosion, shattering Vi, who holds Powder responsible for the terrible loss. Unaware that this act of desertion would have long-term effects on them both, Vi, overcome with sadness and rage, accuses Powder of being a "jinx" and leaves. Powder embarks on a journey of self-destruction and metamorphosis as a result of this separation; in her frailty, she seeks comfort in the evil Silco, who uses her feeling of loss to shape her into the erratic character of Jinx.

Vi and Jinx are moulded by their divergent trajectories over the years: Vi becomes resolute, determined, and dedicated to fighting for justice, while Jinx's innocence turns into instability and volatility. Years later, they reunite in a painful and misunderstood reunion. While Jinx is plagued by her own shattered psyche, struggling with thoughts of betrayal and a desperate longing to be accepted by Vi, Vi wants to reunite with the sister she knew. She is conflicted over her allegiance to Silco, who has taken on the role of a father figure in her life and is advising her to cut off all contact with Powder, her former self. A conflict between family affection and the trauma's lingering wounds is brought to light by Jinx's spiral into chaos and Vi's efforts to save her.

Their relationship and competition highlight important ideas about loyalty and the terrible effects of violence. Jinx, who is both a product of her history and a sad person imprisoned by it, represents the unexpected consequences of trauma, while Vi clings to the notion of family and atonement. With Jinx standing in for the bottled-up rage and bitterness of those who feel abandoned by society and Vi for a desire for reconciliation, their connection mirrors the larger struggle between Piltover and Zaun. Their dynamic's emotional depth and intensity form the emotional centre of Arcane, showing how a single terrible incident may sever ties and have long-lasting effects on loyalty, trust, and identity.

Jayce and Viktor: Creativity and Morality

Although Jayce and Viktor's cooperation is based on mutual respect and ambition, their differing worldviews highlight the moral conundrums that arise when trying to innovate. Hextech is a mystical technology that Jayce, a teenage inventor from an affluent Piltover family, thinks has the potential to transform society and create a better world. A smart but modest assistant with a terminal disease, Viktor views Hextech as a chance to advance the underprivileged, especially the downtrodden Zaun community. Their shared goal of advancement unites them in a potent partnership, despite their disparate reasons.

But as Hextech's potential develops, so do the moral conundrums it raises. Under councillor Mel Medarda's guidance, Jayce develops political clout and begins to understand Hextech's potential as a vehicle for Piltover's power and prosperity. He struggles with the understanding that invention in the wrong hands may result in exploitation and devastation, however, as he digs further into Piltover's political elite and encounters the demands and concessions that come with power. Meanwhile, Viktor becomes irritated with Piltover's council's restrictions on their study. He starts experimenting with Shimmer, a hazardous material that increases Hextech's capabilities but has significant hazards, motivated by his failing health and a desire to transform Zaun. His readiness to cross moral lines serves as an example of the moral price ambition bears when it is tempered by desperation.

Their cooperation begins to deteriorate as Viktor sees no alternative but to go on, even at personal peril, while Jayce leans toward prudence out of concern for the damage Hextech might do. Viktor's increasing seclusion and Jayce's position on the council serve to emphasise their divergent ideologies. Viktor's deteriorating health drives him to take extreme steps in order to realise his vision, while Jayce becomes more and more worried about the political ramifications and social dangers of Hextech. Viktor's covert experiments with Hex Core, a kind of Hextech that interacts with biological matter and may be able to treat his condition, are the result of this conflict. But in the end, his experiments have disastrous results, such as the unintentional death of his aide Sky. Viktor's grief and remorse over her passing highlight the price of unbridled ambition and the sacrifices that are often concealed beneath ground-breaking successes.

The show's examination of the price of advancement and the moral conundrums that come with authority and creativity is reflected in Jayce and Viktor's journey. While Viktor's plunge into dangerous experimentation highlights the possible perils of ambition unbridled by moral reflection, Jayce's political ascent exposes him to the compromises and corruption that may contaminate even the greatest values. Together, they symbolise the paradox of scientific advancement: although it may benefit society, it also has the potential to destroy it if used carelessly. Their storyline serves as a warning to viewers that creativity may have unforeseen and irreparable effects if it is not tempered by empathy and moral discipline.

Vander and Silco: Zaun Leadership

In Zaun, Silco and Vander stand in for two radically different styles of leadership, and the show's examination of treachery, resistance, and power is powerfully metaphorically represented by their divergent worldviews. Due to their shared goal for Zaun's freedom, the two men were once friends in a revolt against Piltover. But they are separated by a profound ideological gap, which turns them from allies into enemies. Disillusioned by the bloody results of their uprising, Vander turns to peace and diplomacy, thinking that stability and compromise are essential to protecting Zaun's future. He becomes a guardian of Zaun's people, attempting to preserve the tenuous peace while utilising his power to keep the undercity safe from Piltover's enforcers.

Silco, on the other hand, adheres to a philosophy of brutality and power and is uncompromising in his pursuit of Zaun's independence. He feels that power is required for Zaun's emancipation, and he is prepared to use any means necessary to accomplish his goal, including the drug trade and the exploitation of weaker people like Jinx. Silco often takes advantage of Zaun's citizens to achieve his own goals because of his fear-based and control-based leadership style. His readiness to employ Shimmer, a hazardous medication that gives superhuman strength but has serious side effects, as an instrument of power is a prime example of his practical, somewhat Machiavellian style of leadership. Silco believes that Zaun's independence is worth every hardship, and he views Vander's diplomacy as a sign of weakness and a betrayal of their common values.

As Silco's desire for Zaun's independence increases, he turns his attention against Vander, intensifying their ideological conflict. As a father figure to Vi, Powder, and other orphans, Vander exemplifies a protective but restrained style of leadership, emphasising life preservation above taking chances with an unknown future. This viewpoint conflicts with Silica's unyielding quest for dominance, which finally results in Vander's apprehension and eventual death in a violent altercation. Their antagonism comes to a head with Vander's passing, which strengthens Silco's hold over Zaun and creates the conditions for Jinx to change under his influence.

Arcane's larger themes of power, corruption, and the difficulty of leadership are echoed in the fight between Silco and Vander. While Silco's brutality appeals to the disillusioned and disaffected who desire for empowerment and retribution, Vander's history as a guardian relates to those in Zaun who crave stability. Their divergent ideas for Zaun highlight the ethical uncertainty of leadership and demonstrate how selfish interests and the brutal reality of life may corrupt even well-meaning principles. The cyclical nature of violence and the heavy price of unwavering ambition are reflected in Silco's eventual death at the hands of his protégé Jinx. Vander's protective tendencies toward Vi and Powder are reflected in his manipulative but sincere paternal affectionate connection with Jinx, underscoring Arcane's complex depiction of paternity and authority.

Arcane offers a potent reflection on the difficulties faced by disadvantaged groups in their quest for autonomy, the moral dilemmas of leadership, and the terrible toll that ideological disputes have on people's lives via Silco and Vander. Their relationship perfectly captures the conflict between resistance and peace, showing how even the most ardent leaders may become corrupted by the pursuit of power, eventually making it difficult to distinguish between oppressor and defender.

Chapter 6

Themes And Symbolism

The conflict between technology and humanity is a recurring topic in Arcane, with Hextech technology serving as both a destructive instrument and a sign of hope. Piltover, known as the "City of Progress," welcomes technology advancement as a way to improve human potential, yet pursuing this advancement raises existential and ethical questions. The world of Arcane exposes a sharp conflict between human morals and technological growth as the city's scientists explore the limits of science and magic and Piltover's council supports Hextech.

Introduced by Viktor and Jayce Talis, Hextech is seen as a positive force. Hextech is seen by Jayce, who attributes his existence to arcane magic, as a way to empower common people and enable them to overcome their limits. His enormous Hex Gates project, which aims to link diverse regions of the planet and transform transportation, reflects this idea. Viktor views Hextech as a means of improving life itself, driven by his own desire to transcend his physical constraints. Piltover is made affluent by their shared vision, but as soon as the elite of Piltover start using the technology for political ends, it enters an ethically dubious area.

The path of Viktor, whose battle with a deadly disease pushes him to drastic methods, best captures the duality of Hextech. Viktor believes that using organic stuff in his research might restore his life, so he changes to Hexcore—a kind of Hextech with transformational capabilities. However, this experiment highlights a moral conundrum: while Viktor's need for survival is very human, it crosses ethical lines, and Sky, his aide, ultimately pays the price. Viktor's tragedy serves as a metaphor for the human cost of unbridled ambition, showing how technology may cause unforeseen misery when it is sought without regard for people.

Hextech is also a prime example of the conflict between Zaun and Piltover, two cities with diametrically opposed attitudes about technology. In Zaun, technology is a symbol of exploitation and power; in Piltover, it is a mark of advancement and status. By developing Shimmer, a deadly substance that gives strength at a high cost, Silco, Zaun's criminal lord, takes advantage of the inequality. Despite being an innovation in theory, Shimmer shows how technology advancements may be used as tools of oppression against underprivileged groups. The contrast between Hextech and Shimmer makes technology seem like a two-edged weapon that can both improve lives and widen social gaps.

Arcane offers a sophisticated examination of the interaction between technology and people using these instances. Silco, Viktor, and Jayce's divergent viewpoints highlight how technology can both inspire and corrupt. Viktor's decline and Silco's weaponization of Shimmer serve as a reminder of the perils of progress when it is divorced from moral and human considerations, despite Jayce's vision of Hextech as a uniting force. In the end, Arcane's warning about striking a balance between creativity and moral responsibility is reflected in this topic of technology vs mankind.

Betrayal, Loyalty, and Family

Arcane's emotional foundation is made up of family, loyalty, and treachery, with the story's focal point being the broken relationship between Vi and

Jinx (previously Powder). Their bond serves as a striking examination of the difficulties of brotherly love and the devastating effects of treachery. The show explores how family ties may influence the lives and motives of the individuals by serving as a source of both strength and deep weakness.

The narrative of Vi and Jinx starts with a strong relationship formed during a traumatic event. As little youngsters, they watch as Piltover's enforcers and Zaunite rebels engage in a bloody conflict, resulting in the deaths of their parents. The sisters are raised in Zaun by Vander, a kind but practical father figure who instils in them a sense of duty and family. Vi takes on the role of protector, vowing to keep her younger sister safe. But on a mission, Powder's desperate attempt to prove herself causes a catastrophic explosion that kills their allies Mylo and Claggor. The moment that characterises their parting occurs when Vi, in a state of sorrow and rage, refers to Powder as a "jinx." Throughout the series, both sisters are plagued by this apparent betrayal, which clouds their judgement in every choice they make.

Silco, who takes on the role of surrogate father to Jinx after Vi's desertion, further explores the concept of loyalty. By taking advantage of Jinx's weakness, Silco feeds her hate toward Piltover and her darker tendencies. Silco uses Jinx's desire for approval to keep her at his side, and he uses loyalty as a tactic to maintain his control over Zaun. The series' portrayal of loyalty is complicated by Silco's sincere concern for Jinx in spite of his cunning. When given the opportunity to guarantee Zaun's independence by giving up Jinx, Silco's decision exposes his moral contradictions. His eventual inability to give her up, even at the expense of his goals, highlights how the series depicts loyalty in a complex way, showing that deception and commitment can coexist.

Loyalty and treachery may appear in partnerships other than Vi and Jinx, especially in Jayce and Viktor's cooperation. They are initially united by their same vision for Hextech, but when their goals change, rifts start to appear. While Jayce, influenced by councillor Mel Medarda, puts Piltover's political stability ahead of personal ties, Viktor's desire to heal his condition drives him to undertake ethically dubious decisions. Their split serves as an example of how ambition and self-interest may undermine loyalty, showing that treachery can happen even in the absence of malevolent intent.

The characters are emotionally affected by these themes, especially Jinx, whose need for family approval marks her spiral into insanity. She pushes Vi to choose between her and Caitlyn in a dramatic moment that culminates her conflicted allegiances to Vi, Silco, and her own fragmented identity. This pivotal scene illustrates the price of treachery and the intense need for loyalty, showing how shattered family ties may cause excruciating pain. In the end, Vi's grief, Jinx's fury, and Silco's warped sense of loyalty illustrate the terrible consequences of treachery and the persistent, sometimes agonising, power of family.

Corruption and Power

A major topic in Arcane is the quest for power, and the show shows how ambition and the need for control can corrupt both people and organisations. Members of Piltover's council, which is supposed to be the epicentre of knowledge and advancement, are shown to be morally reprehensible and eager to take advantage of Hextech for their own political ends. Jayce, who represents the city's slow slide into moral ambiguity, faces the moral concessions that come with power as he advances among Piltover's elite.

Jayce starts off as an idealist who is motivated by the concept that Hextech may be used to advance society as a whole. But his quick ascent to a council post exposes him to the distorting effects of political authority. Mel Medarda, a cunning councillor with her own agenda, helps Jayce understand Piltover's complicated political system. He gives up more of his principles the more he conforms to the council's agenda. Jayce must deal with the unexpected repercussions of his desire at the conclusion of the season, especially when a little kid is killed during an attack on Silco's Shimmer production. Jayce's idea of progress is destroyed by this episode, which shows how pursuing power may weaken one's moral compass.

Conversely, Viktor aspires to control his own fate. Viktor has a fatal disease and is motivated by a personal urge to live, which drives him to do risky experiments on the Hexcore. His desperation and increasing disengagement from his moral principles are seen in his readiness to utilise Shimmer to improve the Hex Core in spite of the possible hazards. As his original goal to use Hextech to improve mankind is overshadowed by a drive to overcome his physical limits at whatever cost, Viktor's shift serves as an example of how personal misery may feed a darker ambition.

In Zaun, where his vicious desire makes him the de facto dictator of the undercity, Silco is a symbol of excessive power and corruption. Silco's goals are less limited by morality than those of Jayce or Viktor. His goal to free Zaun from Piltover's control stems from personal grudges, especially Vander's betrayal of him. In order to solidify his hold on power, Silco uses Zaun's disenfranchised populace and weaponizes Shimmer, assembling an army of chemically empowered enforcers. Silco presents himself as a rebel at first, but his dictatorial reign and readiness to control Jinx and everyone around him exposes his hypocrisy. According to the series, Silco is motivated by a perverted kind of devotion to Zaun that eventually serves his own interests, making him both a victim and a dishonest actor.

Arcane makes a statement on the corrupting influence of power via these characters. For various reasons—idealism, survival, and retaliation—Jayce, Viktor, and Silco all strive for power, but they all end up with compromised morals. The ruling elite of Piltover is a prime example of institutional corruption, where innovation is used to gain power and self-interest takes precedence over fairness. As the city teeters on the verge of conflict at the conclusion of the season, the effects of this corruption become apparent, and people begin to wonder whether the cost of power is too great. Arcane's topic of power and corruption serves as a warning, showing how unbridled ambition may undermine personal morals and cause social instability.

Chapter 7

Visual Style And Animation

Viewers may experience the ambiance of Arcane as if they are roaming the streets of both Piltover and Zaun thanks to the steampunk style, which serves as more than simply a background. This intricate design technique creates a world that is both familiar and foreign by fusing futuristic imagination with aspects of Victorian-inspired equipment. This strategy enables the series to blend industrial themes—such as gears, steam engines, and clockwork mechanisms—with a narrative about the advancement and decline of society, which is a great match for Arcane's thematic weight.

The show uses steampunk elements to create visual contrasts between the undercity of Zaun and the affluent "City of Progress," Piltover. With its sleek shine of cutting-edge Hextech technology, huge glass windows, and polished metals, Piltover's architecture soars. Its imposing, almost cathedral-like structures reflect the wealth and intelligence of its elite. These well-maintained buildings exude a feeling of order, highlighting Piltover's faith in its own advancement and sense of superiority.

Zaun, on the other hand, is portrayed as a dirty, gritty maze of dilapidated buildings, contaminated sky, and dimly lit alleys. Zaun's iron and brass are corroded and worn, while Piltover's metals shine. The city's lowest levels are always hazy with smoke, and its twisting alleyways, small streets, and dilapidated buildings give off an air of claustrophobia and despair. The social and economic division in the series is furthered by this motif; Zaun, in spite of its inventiveness and fortitude, is obviously weakened by neglect, signifying the oppression and exploitation its people face. In addition to reflecting Zaun's suffering, this dark, twisted side of steampunk also highlights the tenacity of its residents, who make due with what little they have and exhibit a creative and unpolished spirit that stands in stark contrast to Piltover's regimented ambition.

The show's struggle between freedom and control, development and exploitation, is given life by the steampunk aesthetic, which also adds conceptual complexity. This is reflected in Zaun's character designs; many undercity individuals have physical modifications or homemade technology that, however ingenious, often draw attention to the terrible reality of their life. Through the use of this aesthetic, Arcane creates a world in which human misery taints scientific advancement, and this struggle is evident in every piece of equipment, metal gear, and brick.

Fortiche's Animation Methods

Arcane was brought to life by Fortiche Productions using innovative animation methods, setting a visual standard that has been hailed as revolutionary by many fans and reviewers. Because of Fortiche's innovative method of blending 2D and 3D animation, Arcane has an almost handcrafted appearance thanks to its textured, painterly feel. With each frame evoking the elegance of classical painting while retaining the energy of contemporary animation, this hybrid approach has distinguished Arcane in the field of animated series.

The skillful blending of 2D and 3D adds depth to the scene while maintaining the sharpness and vibrancy of the foreground items and figures. For some character elements and effects, such as facial expressions, which transmit delicate emotional subtleties and give them an incredibly realistic feel, Fortiche's animators used hand-drawn methods. The delicate hand-drawn lines, for instance, accentuate the emotions of Vi and Jinx in close-up views, portraying everything from the ferocious resolve in Vi's eyes to the tumultuous and tormented gleam in Jinx's. In animation, where computer accuracy may sometimes obliterate the human touch, this attention to emotional detail is uncommon. However, Fortiche combines the tactile warmth of hand-drawn art with this computerised accuracy in Arcane.

Fortiche's technical mastery is on full display in the series' battle sequences. They accomplish a visceral, immersive feel by using dynamic camera motions and 3D models for backdrops. The frenetic intensity of notable scenes, like Vi's fights or Jinx's unpredictable movements, combines stylistic fluidity with fast-paced action. It nearly seems as if the audience can feel every strike as the animation depicts the ferocious fistfights and the unadulterated strength of Hextech explosives. For instance, Jinx's motions are erratic and frantic, indicating her chaotic mentality, whereas Vi's fighting style is animated with hefty, grounded blows, showing her physical strength and no-nonsense attitude.

The bridge duel between Jinx and Ekko is one particularly memorable scene. In order to depict their shared experiences and their current, broken relationship, this scenario alternates between the past and present utilising different visual approaches. The animators give the violent encounter more emotional depth and nostalgia by interjecting bursts of colourful, graffiti-style graphics that symbolise Ekko's recollections of Jinx as Powder. By combining emotional resonance and visual narrative in ways that are uncommon even in high-budget animated projects, Arcane is able to go beyond conventional animation.

Symbolic imagery, colour, and lighting

Arcane relies heavily on colour and lighting, which can act as an unwritten language that expresses tension, mood, and symbolic connotations. Each character's emotional condition and internal problems are depicted by the animators via colour, adding levels of significance to their journeys.

For instance, Jinx is often surrounded by electric blue and purple hues, which represent her spiral into insanity and her change from Powder to Jinx. Her colour scheme represents her instability and addiction to chaos, and it also coincides with the poisonous glow of Shimmer, the hazardous drug that is widely used in Zaun. With its greens and purples, Zaun's vivid neon symbolises the city's tainted beauty and represents Jinx's internal conflict as she vacillates between her violent present and recollections of her innocent past.

Piltover, on the other hand, is often surrounded by warm, golden hues that symbolise its wealth and charm. A visual reminder of Piltover's luxury and the light it shines on the dark undercity below are provided by these sunny sights. However, this radiance often seems cold, implying that underneath Piltover's genius lurks a lack of compassion. Without using words, this well-chosen lighting contrast highlights the power dynamics between Piltover and Zaun.

During pivotal moments, lighting is frequently used to increase tension. Scenes involving treachery, loss, or disclosure are given more emotional weight by the use of deep shadows and strong backlighting. For example, Silco's meetings are often held in complete darkness, with just a little flicker of light highlighting his scarred face, adding to his intimidating appearance. Characters are lighted such that half of their faces are in darkness during emotionally intense scenes, signifying the duality of their decisions and the internal struggles they endure.

Arcane is filled with symbolic imagery that deepens its plot. For instance, the story's recurrent theme of shattered glass symbolises the strained bonds between Vi and Jinx in particular. Broken glass serves as a visual reminder of Powder's fractured mental state and her broken connection with Vi after her catastrophic explosion in Act 1. Hextech crystals represent human ambition and the perilous temptation of development, and they are more than simply sources of power. The crystals' alluring, even mesmerising light symbolises both the terrible potential that comes with unbridled power and promise for a better future.

Scenes featuring Jinx's artwork are when the series' use of visual symbolism reaches its most poignant moment. Her messy personality and enduring commitment to her past are embodied in her graffiti, which is strewn on walls and strewn around Zaun as little details. Between her violent, destructive reality as Jinx and her innocent past as Powder, her work fills the void. Viewers are given a peek of Powder's remaining creativity and desire via her artwork, which stands in sharp contrast to the savagery she portrays.

In Arcane, Fortiche has not only produced a visually stunning show but also a multi-layered, immersive universe in which each component—from animation methods to colour—has a specific narrative function. A masterwork that engages viewers on both an intellectual and emotional level, the series' visual language is as complex as its story, beckoning them to discover every hidden meaning and savour each expertly composed shot.

Chapter 8

Soundtrack And Music

The catchy theme song "Enemy" by Imagine Dragons and JID, which defines the show's emotional and conceptual tone right away, is one of Arcane's most potent features. The dynamic, anthemic rock band Imagine Dragons wrote "Enemy" especially for the show. The lyrics of the song reflect the path of Arcane's characters, especially Jinx, whose feelings of betrayal and mental torment are shown in words like "Everybody wants to be my enemy." "Enemy"'s rhythm, which blends eerie melodies with upbeat rhythms, represents the inner conflicts of individuals divided between ambition and loyalty.

Riot Games and Imagine Dragons have a long history of working together. In 2014, Imagine Dragons and League of Legends collaborated on the song "Warriors," which became an anthem for the League World Championship and became a gaming community icon. This preexisting relationship made "Enemy" more relatable to League of Legends players while also appealing to a wider audience. GOD's involvement gives the song a new level of intensity since his quick lines reflect the frantic but resolute mentality of characters like Vi and Jinx. His unique sound lends the song a rough, urban edge that complements Zaun's grimy underworld. The partnership successfully combines elements of contemporary hip-hop and classical rock, capturing the collision of two worlds: Zaun's unadulterated tenacity and Piltover's luxury.

In addition to Imagine Dragons, Arcane included other gifted musicians including Bea Miller, who helped create the eerily evocative song "Playground." This music instantly creates a gloomy and menacing atmosphere as it introduces viewers to Zaun's grim reality. The air of danger that pervades the city, where surviving is a daily struggle, is captured by Miller's eerie voice. The song acts as an audio entryway into the underworld, capturing the tenacity and despair that characterise Zaun's residents.

Another dimension is provided by Woodkid's "Guns for Hire," whose ominous and symphonic tones reflect the gravity of Piltover's political climate and the moral dilemmas surrounding Hextech. The sombre, almost melancholy tone of the song captures the protagonists' struggles with their decisions and the weight of their goals. Because each song depicts a different aspect of the characters' internal or external struggles, the soundtrack's vast, thematic variety not only reflects the series' intricate world-building but also enhances character depth.

Music's Impact on the Tone of the Series

Arcane's music, which sometimes serves as an unsaid narrator, was painstakingly composed to heighten the emotional impact of each scene. In order to create a soundtrack as complex as the story itself, the series incorporates elements of rock, hip-hop, electronic music, and orchestration. With rock and hip-hop components symbolising Zaun's rebellious nature and symphonic and electronic pieces reflecting Piltover's refined, scientific milieu, this genre fusion reflects the worlds of Piltover and Zaun.

For certain personalities and places, the songs often serve as thematic anchors. For example, the musical compositions that accompany Piltover's council sessions give the city's hierarchical, ordered atmosphere a sense of seriousness and order. Similar to the architectural and cultural characteristics of the city, Piltover's music often prioritises tasteful, well-balanced tones. This is best shown by the music that goes with sequences that feature Jayce and Viktor, whose desire to use Hextech is characterised by upbeat but restrained soundtracks that symbolise Piltover's quest for invention and perfection.

Zaun's scenes, on the other hand, often include distorted melodies, synthetic noises, and deep basslines, giving them a darker, gritty aural quality. Ramsey's song "Goodbye" recalls the danger that exists inside Zaun's boundaries with its eerie vocal line and deep electronic sounds. The sharp contrast between Zaun's gritty, industrial rhythms and Piltover's elegant orchestration not only highlights the cities' separation but also helps viewers better comprehend the cultural conflict.

The way that music is used in Jinx's metamorphosis arc is among the most captivating. Dissonant, eerie songs that mirror her shattered mental condition accompany her psychiatric decline. Songs with jarring rhythms and unsettling vocal lines often highlight her key situations, signifying her fractured identity and descent into madness. Her journey into

Jinx is one of the most memorable character arcs in the series because of the musical selections that enable viewers to viscerally witness her inner agony.

The music not only amplifies the show's emotional pulses but also its conceptual elements, especially the conflict between control and liberation. For instance, the melancholy, reflective music that often accompanies Viktor's episodes reflects his pursuit of transcendence. The slow, sorrowful tunes hint at his unethical concessions in his unrelenting search for a solution and act as a continual reminder of his physical constraints. Arcane establishes a strong connection between sound and narrative by combining certain musical motifs with themes that are centred around characters.

Legendary Songs and Audience Responses

Fans all throughout the globe responded favourably to Arcane's soundtrack, and a few of the songs quickly became legendary. On social networking sites like Twitter and TikTok, "Enemy" gained popularity as fans applauded its compatibility with Jinx's unstable mental state. The song perfectly captured the emotion of being shunned or misunderstood, and many listeners found themselves relating to its themes of loneliness and perseverance. Fan covers, remixes, and animations that praised Jinx's character journey and the greater Arcane world resulted from the song's success. The song's cultural influence in the gaming and music worlds was further shown by Imagine Dragons' live performance of it during the League of Legends World Championship.

Ramsey's "Goodbye" has gained popularity among fans because of its depiction of dread and vulnerability, especially in the parts that deal with Jinx's conflict over her memories of Vi. Fans who saw Jinx as a sad person found solace in the song's ethereal, haunting tones, which create a feeling of loss and loneliness. Discussions over the meaning of the song's lyrics erupted on sites like Reddit and YouTube, where fans saw it as a representation of Jinx's nostalgia for the past and her unwillingness to let go of her early years.

Audiences were particularly enthralled by Bones UK's experimental song "Dirty Little Animals," which plays during a violent fight sequence. Its gritty, defiant vibe came to represent the unadulterated violence seen in Zaun's seedier backstreets. The wild energy of Jinx's pranks was heightened by Bones UK's edgy, unrepentant style, which furthered her character's disdain for social norms. Fans enjoyed how intense this song made action scenes, giving them a visceral rush that raised the action's stakes.

The legacy of Arcane has been greatly influenced by the reaction of the music. The series' ability to build a seamless environment in which music plays a central role in the narrative is often praised by fans. Fans post playlists of their favourite Arcane songs on social media, and conversations on the emotional resonance of the music are frequent. Since the soundtrack effectively conveys the excitement of the environment and increases viewer engagement, some players have even been motivated to learn more about League of Legends mythology. The soundtrack's strong rhythms and emotionally intense lyrics provide a multifaceted experience that goes beyond the screen, making it a doorway into Arcane for many.

The soundtrack has become a milestone in the fan community, and the harmony of Arcane's music and visual narrative has made an enduring impression. The soundtrack is an essential component of the watching experience since it is closely linked to the journeys, aspirations, and changes of the characters. Each track, from the

eerie undertone of "Playground" to the anthemic
call to arms in "Enemy," adds a depth that listeners
can relate to on a personal level, solidifying Arcane
as a ground-breaking accomplishment in both
animation and music.

Chapter 9

Reception And Impact

Arcane has established a new standard for video game adaptations since its inception because of its inventive animation, emotional relevance, and compelling plot. With a distinctive fusion of 2D and 3D animation that embodies the spirit of the League of Legends world while being accessible to new viewers, the series has been praised by reviewers as one of the most aesthetically spectacular programs of its type. Without needing viewers to be familiar with the game beforehand, critics have praised the series' ability to craft a profoundly engrossing story that explores difficult subjects like trauma, family, and social conflicts.

Arcane's record on Rotten Tomatoes, where it has a 100% approval rating and an amazing average score of 9.20 out of 10, has been one of the main markers of its popularity. The series is widely regarded by critics as a game-changer in both animation and video game adaptations, which is reflected in its high rating. Within a week of its debut, Arcane became the highest-rated series on Netflix, ranking first in 52 countries and second in the US. It also set new records on the streaming service.

The accolades Arcane has received attest to its revolutionary influence. As the first video game-based streaming series to win both an Annie Award and a Primetime Emmy Award, the series created history. The series' excellence in a cutthroat market was highlighted when it won the Emmy for Outstanding Animated Program, which was a major accomplishment for Riot Games and Netflix. Another significant milestone for a video game adaptation was reached when Arcane won Best General Audience Animated Television Broadcast Production at the Annie Awards, one of the most coveted honours in the animation business. Additionally, the series won nine Annies, demonstrating its proficiency across a range of animation categories.

In addition to receiving praise from the industry, Arcane took up the Best Adaptation trophy from The Game Awards 2022, a brand-new category designed to recognize the top video game adaptations into other media. This victory cemented its place as a premier adaptation that successfully avoided the infamous "video game curse," which holds that video games are often badly adapted into other media. The IGN review praised Arcane's emotional depth and nuanced characters, calling it "a once-in-a-generation masterpiece." Rafael Motamayor of IGN noted the animation's inventive design and complex world-building, even drawing comparisons to Spider-Man: Into the Spider-Verse.

Arcane pushed the animation industry to think about the possibilities of adult-oriented animated narrative in addition to raising the bar for video game adaptations. Arcane proved that video game mythology could attain cinematic quality and become widely popular if it was treated with narrative care and creative ambition. This was evidenced by the film's critical praise and large viewership.

Reception by Culture and Fans

Arcane struck a deep chord with League of Legends aficionados as well as people who were unfamiliar with the game's world. The show's moral complexity, fascinating characters, and themes of loyalty, personal growth, and belonging are what make it so popular worldwide. Arcane was able to close the gap between League of Legends' current fan base and a larger audience that was not acquainted with the game thanks to its widespread appeal. Indeed, a lot of Arcane fans were taken aback by how effortlessly the series brought them to the League world without requiring them to have played the game beforehand, which is a frequent obstacle in video game adaptations.

Arcane gave League of Legends gamers more nuance to their favourite characters, especially Vi, Jinx, Jayce, and Caitlyn, whose motives and backstories were examined in ways that matched their in-game personalities. From Vi and Jinx Is broken sisterhood to Jayce's moral quandaries about Hextech, the characters' hardships gave well-known personalities new emotional depth. The fan base was revived by this deep narrative, which sparked debates, ideas, and fan art on social media. The intricate depiction of Jinx and Vi's relationship, which was the show's narrative and symbolic core and embodied themes of devotion, betrayal, and family, struck a chord with viewers. Both new and seasoned viewers found the program captivating due to its emotional impact, which drew them into the complex universe of the narrative.

The visual artistry of Arcane was one of its most talked-about features. The show's steampunk-inspired visuals and colourful, intricate settings, which portrayed both Piltover's luxury and Zaun's tough fortitude, enthralled viewers. Fortiche's animation, which blends 2D and 3D components, was praised for its painterly beauty, giving each frame the impression of a painstakingly created work of art. Viewers commended the program for establishing new standards in animated series production, and the emotional intensity was heightened by the attention to detail in facial expressions and movements, particularly during action sequences.

The success of the series was greatly aided by its music. The opening theme, "Enemy" by Imagine Dragons, made Arcane's soundtrack a stand-alone smash. The tone and concepts of the tale were reflected in this song and other songs that were used in the program, which gave the narrative another level of depth. "Enemy" and other soundtrack tracks were swiftly welcomed by fans and became viral on social media sites like Instagram and TikTok, significantly broadening Arcane's cultural influence. Arcane created a multimedia experience that connected with many fan groups by engaging listeners with both music and imagery.

Riot Games' incorporation of Arcane into its ecosystem is another example of how the game has affected the League of Legends fan base. A connection between the program and the games was created by allowing fans to engage with Arcane characters and themes via special events in League of Legends and associated games like Teamfight Tactics and Legends of Runeterra. Because League players believed the program added more depth to the story they had been investigating in the games for years, this cross-platform approach increased fan engagement. In addition to improving the fan experience, this partnership between the game and the series demonstrated the possibilities for multi-platform immersive storytelling.

Impact on Video Game Adaptations and Animation

The animation business has been significantly impacted by Arcane, particularly in regards to the creation, promotion, and reception of animated programs by viewers throughout the world. Studios and streaming services are now more seriously considering video game adaptations, especially in animation, as a viable genre with broad appeal as a result of Arcane's success. Video game adaptations have historically had a challenging journey, with many of them falling short of capturing the spirit of their original content. However, Arcane's success has shown that video game adaptations may not only satisfy but even surpass fan expectations when they have the proper creative vision and narrative commitment.

Raising the bar for visual narrative in animation has been one of Arcane's most important contributions. Riot Games and Fortiche's collaboration has produced a distinctive aesthetic that combines 2D and 3D animation methods, giving the game a rich, atmospheric appearance that is novel and new. Fans and experts in the field have taken notice of this creative approach to animation, which has sparked conversations on how hybrid animation approaches may effectively bring complicated storylines to life. Future animated programs that aim to attain a comparable degree of creative excellence and immersion are held to the same standards as Arcane's intricate and impressionistic graphics.

By appealing to a mature audience without sacrificing depth or maturity, Arcane also defies the norms of animated narrative. Arcane tackles complex issues like social injustice, trauma, and moral ambiguity, making it approachable and relevant for adult audiences in contrast to many animated programs that target children or mostly depend on fantasy clichés. This strategy has changed how people see animation as a medium that can handle intricate, emotionally charged stories in addition to broadening the audience for animated series. Arcane has expanded the possibilities of animated series by addressing topics that are relevant to both individuals and society as a whole. This might lead to the creation of more adult-oriented animated material in the future.

Arcane's legacy has an equally significant influence on video game adaptations. Arcane has upped the bar for future adaptations to honour the original work while adding fresh levels of nuance and emotional connection by crafting a gripping narrative that stands alone. The series has shown that adaptations may explore character-driven tales that enrich the universe created in the games, rather than having to closely follow game mechanics or depend on fan service. This strategy has established a new standard for video game adaptations, pushing companies to prioritise high-calibre production and significant content above immediate financial gain.

Arcane has paved the way for other studios and properties to use animation as a potent tool for growing their worlds, which will have an impact on future adaptations. Due to its popularity, franchises with rich histories and devoted followings could look into comparable adaptations that offer their characters and tales fresh perspectives. Arcane has shown that animated adaptations may appeal to a larger audience in addition to enthusiasts by emphasising character development and visually stunning storyline. The desire for well-executed adaptations has been brought to light by the show's critical and economic success, which may inspire gaming firms to investigate the possibilities of their IPs in a similar way.

Chapter 10

Behind The Scenes

The development of Arcane, a high-stakes project for Riot Games and the French animation company Fortiche, was fraught with difficulties. This was Riot Games' first effort to turn League of Legends into a serialised story that would appeal to both die-hard fans and people who had never played the game before, thus they were breaking new ground from the beginning. Creating a series that could stand alone as an engrossing narrative while delicately incorporating League of Legends' rich backstory was one of the biggest challenges. To strike a balance between offending new viewers and ensuring that devoted followers believed the world was accurately portrayed, careful preparation was necessary.

The production schedule was very demanding; the first season of Arcane took six years to complete. Riot's exacting artistic standards and Fortiche's ambitious animation method, which blended 2D and 3D animation components to produce Arcane's unique, painterly look, contributed to the extension of this period. Because each frame was intended to resemble a hand-painted canvas, the series had a distinct aesthetic that distinguished it from other animated films. This necessitated a great deal of animation method innovation, combining cutting-edge technology and traditional creativity in ways that the animation industry had not yet extensively tried.

Creating the series' distinctive "steampunk" look, which combines science fiction with urban ruin to give Piltover and Zaun life, was another technological difficulty. Within the same series, the graphic design team had to envision and create two very distinct worlds: Zaun's gritty, dark underworld and Piltover's gleaming, Art Deco-inspired technological paradise. It used creative lighting schemes, colour schemes, and ambient design to achieve this paradox and continuously portray the two cities' disparate moods. These visual components raised the story's emotional tone in addition to enhancing its themes of struggle and class inequality.

Importantly, Fortiche used a motion-capture method for character movement, which was then adjusted by hand to preserve an expressiveness and fluidity that are rare in video game adaptations. The procedure made it possible to use subtle facial expressions, which were crucial in capturing the complexity of each character's development. In order to better immerse viewers in the characters' relationships and hardships, scenes were meticulously designed to showcase nuanced facial expressions that carried a great deal of emotional weight. Arcane's ability to elicit authentic feeling from animated characters was praised by critics for its meticulous attention to detail.

Riot Games and Fortiche Work Together

The collaboration between Fortiche and Riot Games was essential to Arcane's success. Due to Riot and Fortiche's prior work together on many League of Legends music videos, there was a degree of confidence and creative freedom that is uncommon in studio partnerships. Riot had a big idea; they wanted a television show that could go deeper into League of Legends characters than just a video game. This called for both a thorough comprehension of the game's backstory and a dedication to character-driven narrative, both of which Fortiche has previously shown in other projects.

Riot's impact was especially noticeable in Arcane's emotional depth and storyline. Arcane placed a more priority on character development and interpersonal interactions than many video game adaptations, which are mostly motivated by action scenes. Fortiche met the problem by concentrating on a cinematic style that used colour, lighting, and atmosphere to portray the characters' emotional states. The immersive experience of League of Legends, where players get emotionally engaged in the characters they control, was paralleled by this kind of visual storytelling.

As Riot and Fortiche sought to produce something unprecedented—a serialised animated series with the production value of a feature film—this partnership stretched the limits of animated television. Riot gave Fortiche a lot of resources, which enabled him to use talent and technology to develop. Riot's reportedly large financial commitment gave Fortiche the freedom to hire a wide range of animators and artists, whose work was crucial to creating Arcane's very polished look. Imagine Dragons contributed the opening theme, "Enemy," and other musicians worked together to create a soundtrack that reflected the series' dark, dramatic, and sometimes sad themes. This dedication also extended to the soundtrack.

Riot and Fortiche pushed these limits in an effort to rethink what was possible in animated narrative as well as to appeal to viewers. Their achievements were acknowledged when Arcane became the first video game-based streaming series to win both an Annie Award and a Primetime Emmy Award, highlighting the Riot-Fortiche partnership's combined success.

Casting and Voice Acting Decisions

The talent pool assembled throughout the Arcane casting process aligned with the series' lofty narrative objectives. Riot Games and Fortiche looked for performers who could provide complicated characters with deep, emotionally charged performances for Arcane. Vi, a woman divided between her sense of justice and her familial devotion, was portrayed by Hailee Steinfeld. Vi was given a combination of toughness and tenderness by Steinfeld's vocal delivery, which captured the unadulterated resolve and contradictory feelings that characterise her path. The series' emotional core is Vi's relationship with

Jinx, portrayed by Ella Purnell. Purnell's portrayal of Jinx, a character who struggles with instability and desertion, gave the role a terrifying complexity. Jinx was one of the most memorable characters on the program because of Purnell's frenetic energy, which alternated between innocence and volatility.

It also paid off to cast Jason Spisak as the main adversary, Silco. Spisak played a nuanced villain who, in spite of his brutality, saw himself as a liberator defending Zaun's freedom. Spisak had to handle a broad spectrum of emotions in Silco's connection with Jinx, where he becomes like a deranged father figure, from manipulation to sincere, if misplaced, devotion. His portrayal enhanced Silco's complexity as a figure who transcends straightforward ideas of right and wrong, emulating the hazy moral boundaries that are essential to Arcane's themes.

Alongside the main cast, supporting characters such as Viktor (voiced by Harry Lloyd) and Caitlyn (voiced by Katie Leung) benefited from powerful vocal performances that deepened the show's multi-layered plot. In contrast to Vi's explosive demeanour, Leung's depiction of Caitlyn provided a composed but resolute presence to the program. Vi's voice quietly expresses Caitlyn's internal struggle between her pity for Zaun's situation and her obligation as an enforcer as they get closer. Viktor was similarly compellingly portrayed by Harry Lloyd, who showed how the character changed from an optimistic scientist to one who was prepared to cross moral lines in the sake of advancement. Viktor was given a subdued intensity by Lloyd's performance, which reflected both his mental toughness and physical weakness.

In order to produce performances that felt authentic and genuine, the voice actors were urged to completely explore the emotional landscapes of their characters. The voice actors improved the show's speech by emphasising these little details, which made the interactions seem as natural as the animation. Arcane stood apart from many other animated programs because of its decision to prioritise character-driven voice acting, which also helped it connect with viewers more deeply. The popularity of the series was largely due to the excellent voice acting, which gave the story's fanciful components a realistic and sympathetic basis.

All things considered, Arcane's success in voice acting was a result of a casting procedure that placed a high value on emotional sincerity. Because each performer contributed a unique viewpoint to their part, the characters seemed complex and relatable. A voice-acting performance that was crucial in solidifying Arcane's status as a revolutionary animated television series was made possible by the combination of expert casting, seasoned performers, and emotionally charged directing.

Chapter 11

Marketing And Global Reach

Riot titles used a ground-breaking cross-platform marketing approach for all of its titles in order to expand Arcane's audience. By leveraging the devoted fan base inside its ecosystem, this strategy produced a smooth transition between the League of Legends realm and Arcane. Known as "RiotX Arcane," the campaign included promos from a number of Riot games, such as Valorant, League of Legends, League of Legends: Wild Rift, Teamfight Tactics, and Legends of Runeterra. These in-game partnerships were thoughtfully crafted to expose players to Arcane's plot and characters while enabling them to engage with the show's components in meaningful ways.

League of Legends, for instance, debuted unique material that was directly influenced by Arcane, such as skins for the main characters Vi, Jinx, Caitlyn, and Jayce, who are essential to the plot of the series. By fusing visual and narrative components with the well-known game mechanics, these exclusive character skins strengthened players' bond with Arcane and provided them with an additional motivation to watch the series. Similarly, Valorant players were rewarded with themed items, such as the "Fishbones" gun buddy, which was a nod to Jinx's famous rocket launcher. The distinction between gameplay and narrative was successfully blurred by these enhancements, which strengthened Arcane's position across Riot's gaming network.

Riot also included exclusive events like challenges and special objectives based on Arcane in Teamfight Tactics and Wild Rift. This improved users' immersion in the universe by enabling them to acquire in-game things while investigating Arcane's themes and characters. Riot Games included players as members of an expanding Arcane fanbase as well as gamers via these experiences. As a consequence, viewers from all of its gaming platforms were invited to immerse themselves in the series via a coordinated, immersive campaign that brought the show's plots to life and produced a multi-layered watching experience.

The effectiveness of cross-platform coordination was further shown by Arcane's November 6, 2021, worldwide debut. In an unusual partnership with Netflix, Riot Games aired the first episode on Twitch, enabling fans to co-stream it and interact with it in real time. This creative tactic drew 1.8 million concurrent viewers on Twitch, making it one of the biggest live-streamed events on the network and generating a ton of interaction from both new users and players.

Partnerships with Different Media

Riot Games collaborated with a variety of other media sources to extend Arcane's reach outside Riot's own platform. Arcane's characters and mythology were introduced to audiences that may not have been acquainted with League of Legends via partnerships with well-known video games such as Fortnite, PUBG Mobile, and Among Us. For example, Jinx became a playable character in Fortnite, a daring crossover that increased Arcane's prominence in one of the most well-known battle royale games globally. This crossover presented Jinx in a fresh, dynamic environment in addition to introducing Arcane to Fortnite's large player audience.

Players were able to access Arcane-inspired content while playing PUBG Mobile thanks to themed events and incentives. Riot's choice to collaborate with PUBG Mobile highlighted the allure of Arcane's action-packed, dystopian themes and struck a chord with players who want engaging, narrative-driven mobile gaming experiences. Similar to this, Arcane-themed cosmetics were introduced in Among Us, giving the game a surprising and entertaining touch. These partnerships, which were individually designed to fit the aesthetic and target demographic of the individual game, opened up Arcane to millions of new viewers and gave fans the opportunity to explore its universe from the perspectives of many other game genres.

Players from other gaming ecosystems were drawn into Arcane's realm thanks to these media agreements, which also helped the game develop a cohesive visual brand. Arcane capitalised on the widespread appeal of Fortnite and PUBG Mobile with these customised partnerships, while also providing League of Legends aficionados with more nuance and interest. Arcane increased its brand awareness by reaching a wider audience and gaming behemoths, turning into a cross-platform cultural phenomenon in addition to a Netflix series.

Activities and Face-to-Face Meetings

Riot Games celebrated the premiere of Arcane by hosting immersive in-person events in addition to in-game promotions, giving fans a hands-on look at the show's environment. The partnership with Los Angeles's Secret Cinema was among the most noteworthy. This live event, which took place on November 21, 2021, gave spectators a firsthand look inside Piltover and Zaun's universe. As characters in a fully realised version of Arcane's world, participants were given "bespoke backstories" and goals. Attendees saw performers in well-known roles as they wandered through carefully designed environments, blurring the lines between audience and character engagement.The immersive event, which combined live-action realism with Arcane's grungy, steampunk aesthetics, was both compelling and unforgettable. In addition to engaging with recognizable characters like enforcers and Zaunite criminals, fans could take part in adventures that mirrored the show's themes of revolt, loyalty, and survival. By allowing fans to post their thoughts and images online, the Secret Cinema event successfully transformed Arcane into a live experience, generating curiosity and attracting new viewers to the series.

Riot Games acknowledged the limits of in-person events due to COVID-19 and pushed Arcane via virtual fan experiences in addition to Secret Cinema. This featured interactive events like digital meet-and-greets, Q&A sessions with the artists, and social media releases of behind-the-scenes information. Even if they were unable to attend in person, Riot's dedication to virtual and hybrid interaction made sure that fans everywhere felt a part of the launch. These online gatherings strengthened the Arcane community by giving many fans a chance to talk with other fans about ideas and characters and by offering a unique look into the series' creation.

In addition to drawing spectators, Arcane developed a fan base that interacted with its universe on many levels by fusing in-game activities, cross-media collaborations, and immersive experiences. In the end, this marketing approach enabled Arcane to evolve from a video game adaptation into a standalone narrative experience that was praised by both League of Legends fans and newcomers.

Chapter 12

Analysis Of Key Episodes

A number of Season 1 episodes are pivotal in Arcane's intricate storyline, interlacing societal topics, character growth, and breathtaking visuals. With a focus on Vi and Jinx, Arcane deftly reveals a complex tale of identity, power, and family, enhanced by pivotal moments that strengthen the viewer's bond with the characters and their hardships. Let's explore these important episodes and see how their key sequences highlight themes and character motives, as well as the series' visually and emotionally striking moments.

Important Episodes and Character Developments

"The Base Violence Necessary for Change" is the *third episode.*
This episode represents the terrible conclusion of Vi and Powder's relationship and a turning point for

both of them. There are tragic fatalities at the end of the explosive scenario as Powder tries to use the stolen Hextech crystals as a weapon in a bid to aid Vi and the gang. In an attempt to prove herself, Powder unintentionally kills Mylo and Claggor and seriously hurts Vander, Vi's favourite character. This visually striking scene, which combines vibrant hues with detonating explosives, marks a symbolic turning point in the story as Powder is reborn as "Jinx." Vi and Powder's separation is solidified in this episode, which sends them down different roads as their mutual trust is irrevocably eroded. It is a visually and narratively powerful event that changes their motives because the exploding imagery captures their emotional repercussions.

"When These Walls Come Tumbling Down" is the sixth episode.
By now, Powder has almost fully changed into Jinx, a figure rife with mental instability, resentment, and shattered memories. A pivotal sequence in this episode between Vi and Caitlyn contrasts Jinx's pain and suspicion with the innocent want for family reunion. As Vi and Jinx eventually get back together, the tension reaches a breaking point as Jinx perceives Caitlyn's presence as a betrayal, revealing her mental decline and mistrust. Flickering hues and close-up views emphasise the

visual discord, which reflects her mental agony and creates a crucial sequence that highlights Jinx's complicated identity conflict.

"The Monster You Created" is episode nine.
A compelling portrayal of broken connections, final betrayals, and decisions that shape destiny can be found in the season finale. Jinx's enjoyment of chaos and retaliation is seen in her symbolic use of the gemstone to craft a lethal rocket that she fires at the Piltover council. In this last scene, Jinx symbolically severs her connection to her old self, symbolising both her spiral into madness and the permanent effects of trauma. This closing scene's visual theme of darkness and vivid neon colours emphasises Vi's devastating awareness of her sister's decline and Jinx's transformation into a villain, adding to the scene's emotional impact.

Moments That Have an Emotional and Visual Impact

Arcane creates powerful, emotionally charged images by combining steampunk style with incisive animation. Using a distinctive colour scheme, contrasting shadows, and vibrant animation, pivotal scenes like Jinx's first violent outburst in *Episode 3,* her reunion with Vi under the eerie neon lights in *Episode 6,* and her turn into a villain in

Episode 9 showcase her psychological development. By emphasising each pivotal moment and shedding light on the characters' nuanced motives and internal conflict, these images raise the emotional stakes.

Breakdown by Act

Each of the three acts that make up Arcane's story raises the stakes and develops the character arcs. With each act setting the stage for increased tension and character changes, this act structure does more than just divide episodes; it establishes a rhythm that propels the story into its climax moments.

Act 1: Forming Relationships and First Conflicts

Piltover and Zaun are presented in Act 1 as two different worlds, one characterised by wealth and creativity and the other by poverty and disobedience. The link between Vi, Powder, and their father figure Vander is the main emphasis of this act, which also lays the foundation for the underlying struggle between the oppressed people of Zaun and the elite of Piltover. Here, we see Vi's protective tendencies and Powder's fears and need for approval—themes that would fuel their future disputes.

Character Developments: Powder's weakness and willingness to help contrast with Vi's stern, protective demeanour, illustrating their connection as one based on flimsy dependency but intense commitment. As a father figure, Vander provides a sense of security and familial ties, demonstrating the importance of love and selflessness in the Zaunite way of life, particularly when he gives his life for Vi and Powder in the episode three climax.

Act 2: Growing Disagreement and Change

Act 2 examines how both sisters develop and change as a result of opposing forces. Under Silco's tutelage, Powder recasts herself as Jinx, a frenzied and impetuous character moulded by her fears and Silco's manipulations. Vi, on the other hand, eventually comes to the realisation that making amends with Powder would be more difficult than expected and teams up with Caitlyn, Piltover's enforcer.

Creating Tension: Every Act 2 episode intensifies the tension between Piltover and Zaun while driving Vi and Jinx closer to a collision path. The Act explores the emerging Hextech technology of Jayce and Viktor, comparing Zaun's dependence on unreliable, raw resources like Shimmer with Piltover's scientific advancement.

Symbolic Moments: Powder's baptism by Silco as "Jinx," in which he leads her to the river where Vander attempted to drown him, is a symbolic gesture that simultaneously embraces and destroys her purity by severing her previous links to her family. Flickering lights, vibrant hues, and fragmentary memories are visual representations of her increasing instability.

Act 3: Momentous Meetings and Disclosures

The ideological disputes between Piltover and Zaun crescendo in Act 3, as Vi's desperate attempt to preserve Powder clashes with Jinx's unruly mayhem. Vi's heartbreaking realisation that she cannot "save" her sister and Jinx's eventual acceptance of her new identity are the results of this deed. This last deed reveals the wider societal repercussions of the sisters' decisions while highlighting their terrible parting.

Act 3's narrative and emotional culmination is unvarnished and metaphorical. Jinx uses the stolen gemstone to create a weapon that represents her anguish and rage, completing her metamorphosis. The unbridgeable abyss of distrust and severed familial connections is symbolised by the tension between Vi, Caitlyn, and Jinx, who views Caitlyn as an invader in her relationship with Vi. Intense images, deep shadows, and striking colour contrasts highlight the emotional destruction each character experiences at the act's conclusion in Episode 9.

Emotional and Symbolic Turning Points

Arcane's emotional and symbolic climaxes heighten the series' examination of power, family, and identity. In addition to being emotional high points, key scenes are also turning points that alter themes and character trajectories.

Scenes of Emotional Climax and Their Significance

Episode 3's Explosion
Powder's catastrophic detonation symbolises her symbolic fall from innocence and captures her inner agony and longing to be appreciated by her sister. Her conduct, which was motivated by a need for approval, has disastrous results and destroys her family and self-esteem. In addition to confirming Vi's belief that her sister is a "jinx," this incident lays the groundwork for Powder's ultimate transition into Jinx. The broken crystals, the blue

colour of the explosion, and the eerie aftermath all represent Powder's shattered innocence and the unchangeable course she has chosen for herself.

Jinx's baptism in the river in Episode 5

Powder's new identity is cemented by Silco's act of "baptising" her as Jinx beside the river, a location that has memories of treachery and near-death experiences for him. This moment is full of metaphorical meaning: the river represents death and rebirth, while Silco's manipulation of Jinx demonstrates his psychological dominance over her. As Jinx struggles with her allegiance to Silco and her enduring love for Vi, the colour scheme changes to deeper, more sinister hues, perfectly expressing the depth of her inner turmoil.

Episode 9's Final Showdown

In the season's emotionally intense and symbolic climax, Vi, Caitlyn, and Jinx square off against one another in a run-down warehouse, a suitable setting that symbolises the shattered remains of their history. The colours, lighting, and quick cuts in the sequence reflect Jinx's shattered mental state as she tries to make Vi decide between herself and Caitlyn. The moment is made more difficult by Silco's presence, especially given his paternal devotion for Jinx. Jinx's symbolic launch of the gemstone-powered rocket at the conclusion of the episode shows that she has come to terms with her new role as a force for chaos and devastation.

Characters' Persistent Emotional Impact

Each character is affected emotionally by these culminating events. The enduring effects of pain and devotion are shown by Jinx's battle with her fragmented identity, Caitlyn's fortitude as an outsider pushed into a foreign environment, and Vi's desperate attempt to regain her sister. Intense imagery and themes, such as broken crystals and menacing shadows, highlight each climax, lending weight to the series' examination of identity, loss, and the search for belonging.

Arcane's narrative depth is increased by this structure of crucial scenes, act-by-act development, and symbolically rich climaxes, which produces a nuanced and emotionally impactful depiction of intricate individuals and relationships set against a vividly imagined environment.

Chapter 13

Legacy And Future Of Arcane

Season 2 of Arcane has created a great deal of expectation since the previous season ended on a cliffhanger and captivated both League of Legends world enthusiasts and those who were not familiar with it. Season 2 will examine the fallout from Jinx's bombing of Piltover's council chamber, raising concerns about the whereabouts of council members Jayce, Mel, and Heimerdinger, whose survival is in doubt. A violent escalation between Piltover and Zaun is set in motion by the bombing council meeting, which had the potential to bring about peace between the two communities. This poses important queries about the next second season: Will Piltover pursue retribution? Will Jinx's chaotic influence cause Zaun to launch a full-scale revolt, or is there anybody who can mediate a peaceful resolution?

Season 2 will also see a strong resonance of the identity topic as Vi struggles with her dual roles as Jinx's sister and an enforcer. Vi will have to decide between her devotion to Piltover's shaky order and her love for her estranged sister. She will also have to consider how Caitlyn could affect Vi's choices. In the midst of this chaos, Ekko and the Firelights represent resistance and optimism, with Heimerdinger's help—who could utilise his expertise to help Zaun's underbelly. The technology divide between the cities could close as a result of Heimerdinger and Ekko's possible collaboration, forging unanticipated partnerships.

Season 2 will see a deeper development of character arcs, especially via the experiences of Vi, Jinx, and Caitlyn. Because of Jinx's severe metamorphosis brought on by Silco's influence, Vi will have to consider whether Powder, the sister she knew, can even be saved. In the meanwhile, Caitlyn takes on a personal grudge that may be sparked by the death of her family, particularly if Cassandra Kiramman did not make it out alive from the council explosion. Caitlyn's character would be given more complexity by this retribution narrative, which may also challenge her desire to enforce Piltover's rules in the face of personal pain while also perhaps bringing her closer to Vi.

Prolonged Impact on the League of Legends World

In addition to giving life to characters like Vi, Jinx, and Heimerdinger, Arcane has significantly changed and expanded League of Legends' narrative since its release. By effectively bridging the gap between the game and its expansive world, Arcane has improved fan comprehension and given well-known heroes new emotional dimensions. Viktor's tale, for instance, emphasizes his transformation from a kind inventor to a potentially tragic monster, especially his obsession with the Hexcore. Players' connection to Viktor's character journey is strengthened by this examination of his decline, which also adds to the game's thematic richness by connecting with his past in League of Legends mythology.

The intricate sociopolitical environment between Piltover and Zaun has also been shown to viewers via the program. The League community has been inspired to go beyond individual champions and take into account the larger, systemic challenges inside the game's environment by this emphasis on class divide, ethics in technological development, and the battle for power. The League universe's narrative potential is now enhanced by adult topics like corruption, betrayal within the family, and ideological conflicts, which Arcane has shown can be addressed in Runeterra storylines. Given Arcane's success, Riot Games may use it to craft more complex plots for upcoming events or brand-new lore-based content, allowing players to revisit well-known heroes in these themed settings.

Fans are wondering about possible crossovers into other media genres, since Arcane has also established a precedent for League of Legends' artistic style. The show has shown that animation can effectively convey meaningful storylines, and it may serve as an inspiration for future projects like animated versions of other League champions or geographical areas. The community has discussed investigating areas such as Demacia or Ionia, which might emphasize themes like honor, justice, and cultural conflict while showcasing each region's own features within Runeterra.

Prospects for Upcoming Modifications

Fans now anticipate more character-driven League of Legends television shows as a result of Arcane's enormous success, which has raised the bar for game-to-screen adaptations. The popularity of the series demonstrates the high level of interest in in-depth analyses of the lives of champions from different League areas, each of them has a unique past and set of struggles. Other versions that concentrate on areas such as Noxus, Ionia, or Shurima are thus now seen as promising approaches to examining the ethical and political complexity of these worlds. For instance, a Noxus-focused adaption would explore its culture of military ambition and include heroes like Darius and Swain, while also examining their connections to power and conquest.

The industry's expectations for animated adaptations, particularly those based on video games, have increased as a result of the positive reaction given to Arcane's narrative complexity and animation style. Riot Games and Fortiche have shown with Arcane that animated shows can successfully combine complex narrative with high-octane action, winning praise from both reviewers and general audiences. Arcane is a groundbreaking production that has paved the way for other video game properties, maybe encouraging companies to rethink their own adaptations with a fresh emphasis on visually inventive and character-driven narrative.

There is a clear need for further adaptations set in the League world. Many fans would want to see an adaptation that focuses on Shurima's ancient heritage and ascent to power, or champions like Yasuo and Ahri brought to life in tales that depict the spirituality and mysticism of Ionia. Themes like heritage, atonement, and the struggle between traditional magic and contemporary strife might all be explored in such a series. In the end, Arcane has laid the groundwork for further adaptations that push the limits of game-based narrative while also broadening the reach of League of Legends.

Made in United States
Troutdale, OR
12/19/2024

26949429R00066